我喜欢上托儿所

I LOVE TO GO TO DAYCARE

作者：谢莉 · 阿德蒙特
插图：索娜 · 戈亚尔和苏米特 · 萨库加

www.kidkiddos.com

support@kidkiddos.com

Second edition

Translated from English by Xiaochi Sun
翻译：孙晓池
Chinese editing by Rongrong Wang
王容容 中文校译

Library and Archives Canada Cataloguing in Publication
I Love to Go to Daycare (Chinese English Bilingual Edition)/ Shelley Admont
ISBN: 978-1-5259-3983-9 paperback
ISBN: 978-1-77268-681-4 hardcover
ISBN: 978-1-77268-679-1 eBook

Please note that the Chinese and English versions of the story have been written to be as close as possible. However, in some cases they differ in order to accommodate nuances and fluidity of each language.

献给那些我最爱的人

For those I love the most

吉米躺在床上，抱着他最喜欢的泰迪熊。他试着入睡，可是总有什么东西困扰着他，让他睡不着。

Jimmy was lying in his bed hugging his favorite teddy bear. He was really trying to sleep, but something bothered him and kept him wide awake.

他翻身下床去找他的爸爸妈妈。

He rolled out of bed and went to look for his parents.

在楼下的客厅里，他的爸爸和妈妈正在看电视。吉米抱着他的泰迪熊坐在妈妈的膝盖上。“妈咪，我睡不着。”他说。

Down in the living room, his mom and dad were watching TV. Holding his teddy, Jimmy sat on Mom's lap. "Mommy, I can't sleep," he said.

妈妈揉着他的头发，给了他一个吻。
“你在想什么呢？”

Mom ruffled his hair and gave him a kiss. “What are you thinking about?”

“我在想托儿所的事情。”他小声说，
紧紧的抱着妈妈。

“I’m thinking about daycare,” he whispered and hugged Mom tightly.

“噢，亲爱的，托儿所很有趣的！”妈妈说。

“Oh, sweetie, daycare is so fun!” said Mom.

“你会在那里遇到新的朋友，” 爸爸补充道，
“事实上，托儿所真是太有趣了，
我希望我也能去！”

“You’ll meet new friends there,” added Dad. “In fact, it’s so much fun that I wish I could go, too!”

“我能待在家里和你们在一起吗？”吉米问。
他把头靠在妈妈的肩上。

“Can I stay at home with you?” asked Jimmy. His head fell on Mom’s shoulder.

妈妈轻轻地抚摸着他的头，深深的看着他的眼睛。

Mom stroked his head, looking deeply into his eyes.

“你看这样如何，”她说，
“因为这是你去幼儿园的第一天，
你就只在那儿待两个小时。之后，我就来接你回家。
但是我肯定你在那里会玩得很开心的，
甚至于你都不想离开那儿。”

“How about this," she said. “Since it’s your first day in daycare, you’ll only stay there for two hours. After that, I’ll come back to take you home. But I’m sure that you'll have so much fun that you won’t even want to leave.”

“你知道吗？”爸爸说，
你还可以带着你的泰迪熊。听起来不错吧，
小伙子？”吉米点点头。

“You know what?” said Dad. “You can even take your teddy bear with you. Does that sound good, champ?” Jimmy nodded.

“噢，你真是个聪明的男子汉，”妈妈柔声说道，并亲吻了他的额头。“你一定累了，我们去睡觉吧。”

“Oh, you're such a big and smart boy,” said Mom, kissing his forehead. “I'm sure you're tired. Let's go to bed.”

她把吉米带到他的卧室，并把他放在被窝里。然后，她给了他一个晚安之吻，并在他的耳边轻轻说：“我爱你，亲爱的”。

She led Jimmy to his room and tucked him in. Then, she gave him a goodnight kiss and whispered in his ear, “I love you, sweetie.”

“我也爱你，妈妈。”吉米说。打了一个大哈欠后，他抱着他的泰迪熊闭上了眼睛。

“I love you too, Mom,” said Jimmy. With a big yawn, he hugged his teddy bear and closed his eyes.

就在吉米要睡着的时候，他听到了一个奇怪的声音。“嘿，吉米！”

Jimmy was almost asleep when he heard a strange voice. “Hey, Jimmy!”

他睁开眼睛，看看四周。“谁在说话？”吉米喃喃的说。

He opened his eyes, looking around. “Who’s talking?” murmured Jimmy.

“是我，你的泰迪熊！”

“It’s me, your teddy bear!”

吉米吓了一跳，向下一看。泰迪熊摆着手在微笑。“我知道你很心烦。”泰迪熊说。

Astonished, Jimmy looked down. The teddy bear waved his hand and smiled. “I saw you were upset,” said the teddy bear.

J

吉米深深的叹了一口气。“是啊，我明天要去托儿所。”他咕哝着。
Jimmy sighed deeply. “Yes, I’m going to daycare tomorrow,” he mumbled.

“吉米，我的朋友，可我会跟你一起去的！”泰迪熊向吉米眨眨眼睛，又给了他一个大大的泰迪熊式微笑。”
“Jimmy, my friend, but I’m going with you!” The teddy bear winked at Jimmy and gave him his big teddy-bear smile.

吉米看着他跳来跳去，还拍着手，忍不住哈哈大笑起来。
Jimmy looked at him jumping and clapping and burst out laughing.

“嘘···”泰迪熊小声说。他指指吉米的两个正在睡觉的大哥哥。
“Shhhh,” whispered the teddy bear. He pointed to Jimmy’s two older brothers, who were sleeping in their beds.

他跳到吉米的怀里，紧紧的依偎着他。“晚安，我的朋友！”
He jumped into Jimmy's arms and cuddled him close. "Goodnight, my friend!"

第二天早上，吉米的两个哥哥跳下床走到他的身边。

The next morning his two older brothers jumped out of bed and walked over to Jimmy.

“今天是你上托儿所的第一天，你真幸运。”他的大哥哥说。

“Today is your first day in daycare. You are so lucky,” said his oldest brother.

吉米很兴奋，又有一点担心。“我今天只去两个小时，”他喃喃地说，“这时间很长吗？”

Jimmy was excited but a little bit worried. “I’m only going for two hours today,” he murmured. “Is it a long time?”

“不怎么长。”他的大哥哥说。

“你都没待到睡午觉的时候。”二哥哥补充道。

“Not really,” said the oldest brother.

“You won’t even stay for a nap,” added the middle brother.

早餐时候吉米很安静。“你准备好要走了吗，吉米？”在他吃完盘子里的东西后，妈妈问道。

During breakfast Jimmy was very quiet. “Are you ready to go, Jimmy?” Mom asked, after he cleared his plate.

“我猜是吧。”他低头看着他的泰迪熊，回答道。

“I guess,” he answered looking down at his teddy bear.

泰迪熊给了他一个大大的微笑，吉米感觉好多了。

The teddy bear gave him a big smile and Jimmy felt much better.

J

他一只手拿着他的泰迪熊，另一只手牵着妈妈的手，然后他们出发了。

He took his teddy bear in one hand and Mommy's hand in the other and they set out.

“你会喜欢的，宝贝，”在他们一起走的时候妈妈说，“两个小时后我就回来接你，就在点心时间过后。”

"You'll like it, honey," said Mom while they were walking. "And I'll be back in two hours, right after snack time."

“我知道，妈妈。我很好，我带着我的泰迪熊呢。”吉米冲他的泰迪熊眨眨眼。

"I know, Mommy. I'm fine. I have my teddy bear with me." Jimmy winked at his bear.

“我真为你骄傲，我的男子汉。”妈妈边说边走向托儿所的门。

"I'm so proud of you, my big boy," said Mom as the pair walked up to the daycare's door.

妈妈敲了两下门，一位女士出现在门前。
Mom knocked twice, and a lady appeared at the door.

“你好，吉米，”女士说，“我们在等你呢，快进来！”
“Hello, Jimmy,” the lady said. “Come on in!”

“她怎么认识我的？”吉米悄悄地问他的妈妈。
“How does she know me?” Jimmy whispered to his mom.

妈妈笑了。“我之前给她打过电话，告诉了她我们要来。”
Mom smiled. “I called her before and told her we were coming.”

他们来到一个又大又明亮的房间，那儿有很多其他小孩儿。他们中的一些在玩玩具车，还有一些在玩洋娃娃。
They came into a large, bright room. There were a lot of other kids there. Some of them were playing with cars, and others were playing with dolls.

我们也去玩吧，来吧，吉米！”泰迪熊笑着说。吉米转向他的妈妈。

“Let’s go have some fun. Come on, Jimmy!” the teddy bear said. Smiling, Jimmy turned to Mom.

“去玩吧，亲爱的，”她说，“点心时间过后我来接你。”

“Go have fun, sweetie,” she said. “I’ll pick you up right after snack time.”

“我记得呢。拜拜，妈妈！”吉米一边喊着一边跑去玩一个大玩具卡车。

“I remember. Bye, Mom!” Jimmy yelled as he ran to play with a large truck.

两个小时后，妈妈回到托儿所来接吉米。他跑去见妈妈，并且给了她一个大大的拥抱。

After two hours, Mom came back to the daycare to pick up Jimmy. He ran to meet her and gave her a huge hug.

“妈妈，这儿真的很好玩！”他大声说，“我玩了大卡车，还画了一朵花给你，是我自己画的！”

“Mom, it was so much fun!” he shouted. “I played with a large truck, and then I painted a flower for you all by myself!”

妈妈高兴的笑着：“真的是好漂亮啊。你今天还做什么了？”

Mom smiled happily. “It’s so beautiful. What else did you do today?”

“老师给我们读了一本书，之后我们还吃了点心。”吉米一口气说道，跳到妈妈旁边。

“The teacher read us a book, and after that we ate a snack,” Jimmy said in one breath, bouncing near Mom.

“明天我能多待一会儿吗？求你了，妈妈！”

“Can I stay for longer tomorrow?
Please, Mom!”

第二天，他待得比前一天久。第三天，他待得更久了。现在。

The next day, he stayed longer. The day after that he stayed even longer.

吉米一整天都在托儿所里度过，并且玩的很开心！他喜欢玩游戏、画画，听故事还有吃东西。

Now, Jimmy spends the whole day in daycare having lots of fun! He loves to play games and paint, to hear stories and eat.

午睡时间到了，他也很高兴，因为他可以休息一会儿了。

He is also happy when naptime comes, so he can rest a little bit.

有时候吉米并不带着他的泰迪熊。

Sometimes Jimmy doesn’t bring teddy bear with him.

但是每天他回到家的时候，他会把当天发生的所有事情都讲给他听。

But when he comes back home from daycare, Jimmy tells him all about his day.

www.ingramcontent.com/pod-product-compliance
Lightning Source LLC
LaVergne TN
LVHW071727230826
846093LV00024B/541

* 9 7 8 1 5 2 5 9 3 9 8 3 9 *